The Three Keys To A
Truly
Happy
Retirement

Tripp Thompson

Copyright © 2013 Tripp Thompson
All rights reserved.

ISBN: 1479182699
ISBN 13: 9781479182695
Library of Congress Control Number: 2012915850
CreateSpace Independent Publishing Platform
North Charleston, South Carolina

Introduction

The unknowns of life can be puzzling at times. Many of us are taught about the American dream as children and seem to chase that dream well into our later lives. Most take varied, winding paths and the majority end up short of true happiness. We are taught that to be happy in retirement you need a financial number: a large account balance or nest egg that anyone would recognize as successful. I am truly convinced that this myth is a cloudy guess at the truth to retiring truly happy. I've been blessed to be in the financial planning business for more than fifteen years. I worked as an investment broker early in my career. Today the term is *financial advisor*. For the past decade, I've traveled the East Coast, primarily working as a representative for mutual-fund companies, variable-annuity companies representing variable and fixed annuities from companies you have all heard of. My job entails helping financial advisors and their clients figure out how these products work and if they may be a fit for certain clients and their retirement plan. For a large part of my career, God has blessed me through my meeting and working with an amazing number of wonderful, honest, and ethical people. I've always felt we took the high road in selecting the right products for the right situation. I also, however, felt God was calling me, speaking to me to do more to help people. It seems that God shapes us like the walls of the Grand Canyon: slowly, accurately, and totally at his pace, not ours. There were a series of events that I feel were integral to God's shaping me for what I'm doing today. I hope your walk with me through these events will help you understand the clarity of purpose that I possess and the learning that has led me to share these *3 Keys to a Truly Happy Retirement* with you.

chapter

ONE

The Hardest Lesson

How many of you remember when your children were very young? The blessings of small children are incredible, but those blessings are hard work. As a traveling husband with a very demanding career, I'm slightly ashamed to admit how much my wife did to raise our two wonderful children as she withstood lack of sleep, diapers, temper tantrums, food frenzies, and more. I am truly not worthy of the woman God has provided as my wife. As with most young families, a real vacation without the kids was a far-fetched dream. Fortunately, we got a reward trip through my employer at the time, and received the invitation to spend a week in Cabo San Lucas, Mexico…without the kids. Our problem was that

Tripp Thompson

we lived hours away from our nearest relatives, so we usually did not have access to overnight help with the children. After a few months of planning, my wife's mother decided she would and keep the kids, so we could go on the vacation. My wife's parents own a modest home on a piece of family land with a large pond in the front yard. Their property requires constant attention, as does their pet dog, so my wife's father agreed to stay home in order to take care of things. He is a notorious "project" man, so he had plenty to keep him busy while his wife stayed with the grandchildren. Though my mother-in-law was in good health, she had diabetes; we had real concerns about this being too much on her, but, after hours of discussion, she reassured us she would be fine, and that we would be crazy not to go on the trip. So, the time came for us to leave. We had everything laid out for her from meals to maps to preschool schedules.

We were off! After a connecting flight in Texas, we finally landed in Mexico about nine hours after we had left the East Coast. We thought were there. Another two hours in customs, a one-hour bus ride to our hotel, and we had finally made it. We got to our room, changed, freshened up, and headed down to dinner with our friends and coworkers. It was so windy that one of the buffet tables blew over at dinner, making it difficult to have any conversations with our friends. We all laughed, shook our heads, and said, "See you at breakfast." After a day of traveling and months of being with two children under the age of five, we were tired. We thought a few nights of undisturbed sleep would be pure heaven. We got back to our beautiful room, which was pitch-dark black because we had turned on no lights when we arrived, and the stormy weather allowed no moonlight. There was only one thing we could see when we entered the room: a small, flashing red light.

As with most hotel rooms, the flashing light meant there was a message waiting. As tired as we were, all we hoped was that we had a message about a massage, a manicure, a tee time, or something along those lines of peace and relaxation. What I heard when I pushed the red button would forever change our lives, plans, and career. The message was the following:

"Kids, it's your mom. I hope you get this soon, because your father has had a heart attack. He has been life-lighted to Providence hospital in

Tripp Thompson

Columbia, South Carolina, and I have no more details right now. I've gotten the children out of preschool, and we are driving to the hospital now. We should be there in another three hours. Please, if you get this message and this is not the Thompson room, can you please help me this to them? The lady at the hotel did not speak very fluent English, and I am hoping this is the right room."

The hardest thing to do after a message like that is to hold your wife, hand her the phone, and then support her as she gets crushed about something that painful about her father. The range of emotions she felt was wide and traumatic. She had thoughts like, "Did I tell him I loved him? Does he know how much he means to me? Does he know we need him? Will he be okay? Will I ever see him again?" Quick life lessons for us all here: *do not wait!* Tell your loved ones now and every time you see them or speak with them how much you love them. We never know what each day brings, so why chance it? Here it is: full disclosure. My father-in-law and I are close, extremely close. I love him, and I can't tell you how much he's accepted my coming into his family and marrying his only daughter. I obviously had the same questions my wife did about our last conversations, meetings, history, and so on, but I must admit there was a single thought, a question based on my profession that I did not know the answer to and absolutely had to find out. You see, my father-in-law is retired from the United States army, and he has a military pension. Because he's always been incredibly humble and private about all things financial, I had never asked about his pension election or any other financial matters. It all hit me at once. Oh God, what if he dies and had chosen a single-life pension instead of joint-life? Will my mother-in-law be okay? Will she have enough money each month to live on comfortably and pay someone to take care of the home, the land, the pond, and the dog? You see, my mother-in-law is retired from civil service, but also has diabetes, as I mentioned earlier. She is not physically able to do any moving, lifting, raking, mowing, and so on. These are real concerns, and as a financial advisor, these are things that I knew could become real-life problems in the first thirty days of a surviving spouse's new situation; however, all these thoughts, emotions, and tears do not help you when you are stuck somewhere and waiting. They pull at your heart and they play with

Tripp Thompson

your emotions like a cat with a ball of string. This was the longest, hardest, day of my life. After the help of a few wonderful friends and coworkers, we got to the hospital in South Carolina twenty-four hours after we had first received the voicemail. When we arrived at the hospital, we met my wife's mother in the cardiac intensive care unit, and were scared to death to see what had happened while we were traveling. Turns out God had decided it wasn't quite his time, and, after an emergency triple-bypass surgery and some other cardiac work, my father-in-law was considered to be in serious but stable condition. The sheer joy and emotion we felt at knowing we were going to see him, kiss him, and tell him we loved him made the pain virtually disappear. There was no way my wife was leaving that hospital without her dad. As happy as we were that he had survived, I still had this burning question that I needed answered. I waited patiently until we had all met with the doctor, got our last update of the night, and then it happened.

I pulled my mother-in-law off to the side, and I asked her, "Are you going to be okay?"

She said, "I'm better now and realize we have a lot to do to help him recover."

The Three Keys to a Truly Happy Retirement

I followed up. "I don't think I asked you the proper question. I need to know if you need anything monetarily. We are here for you one hundred percent. Are you going to be fine in the future if something happens again and he doesn't survive?"

She smiled at me and said, and I quote, "When he retired from the army, he thought he would not live to be very old, because his father passed away at age sixty-two. He decided to take the joint-life pension payout, so that I would always have a paycheck, even if he wasn't around. When I retired from civil service, we decided that I would take the single-life payout, so that I would have another paycheck each month for as long as I'm alive."

"Son, she said, "He built our house from the ground up on family land. We have always lived very modestly and never believed in having debt. You do not have to worry about money and me. We are just fine."

There it was, the albatross in the room had been asked and answered, and I was blown away by the comfort and confidence of my mother-in-law's response. Her only concern was taking care of her husband and helping him get well again. I'm a firm believer that he is still alive today and doing well because of a couple of things:

1. God said it was not his time!

2. Great medical technology and trained professionals did their jobs beautifully.

3. That a helicopter picked him up and got him quickly to the right care when he was in medical trouble.

4. Their ability to be financially conservative while having two guaranteed paychecks every month.

The comfort of no debt and guaranteed income allowed my mother-in-law to devote her time and energy to the mission of helping her husband get well. They walked together, shopped together, traveled together, and ate healthier together because they were (and are) committed to each other's well being. She had the commitment and the ability to love and help him. Over eight years have passed since this happened, and I've never seen a happier retired couple in my life. The event was life-changing for my in-laws, but it has also helped me gain a true understanding of what I have observed in my profession that has led me to write this book. Since this happened back in 2004, I have been on a professional and spiritual mission to share this story, to learn from other retirees, and to ask the questions to facilitate the comfort and protection of others. How many people have these concerns but just don't know how to ask them? How many people meet with their bank or financial advisor and get so caught up in details and technical discussions about markets and interest rates that they spend the entire meeting on this and never get to the real questions about what is important? We have to change the conversation and show people that protecting their lifestyle in retirement—no matter what life throws at them—is really the main goal and objective. We like to think we know what life may bring, but we really don't. Only God does. My father-in-law had his heart attack at the same age that his father passed away. He thought past events would play out for him in a similar fashion, and they almost did, but God wasn't ready or him.

God was working his magic and putting his touches on all our learning and understanding and actually making us all a better family for it. Without this near tragedy, I would not have the passion and purpose that it taught me.

Now we move into the specifics of the *3 Keys to a Truly Happy Retirement*. I hope you feel like you are getting a clear picture so far of how these circumstances have already impacted my in-laws.

How would my mother-in-law have handled this situation if she had no idea what would happen to her income or what her monthly budget would be? How would she have handled this if they had been burdened with debt?

chapter

TWO

The 1ˢᵗ Key of a *Truly* Happy Retirement:

SUFFICIENT

GUARANTEED

INCOME

Let's begin by exploring some lessons I learned in the last decade of my financial career. After the stock market downturn of the early 2000s, many Americans were asking hard questions about their lives, financial security, and family situations. As if the tech stock bubble bursting were not enough stress for most people, the events of September 11, 2001, turned personal searching and questioning on its end. The meetings, planning, emotions, reassurance, and the like for financial advisors and their clients reached a new level of depth. For many people, this was a great thing, as they now had someone who helped them with their investing. The problem was that many of these people truly had no personal emotional connection with their advisors. For almost twenty years after President Ronald Reagan was sworn in, our country and our stock markets had the most magical run in a century. From 1980 to 1999 was most likely the greatest twenty-year run for stocks that we've ever seen in the history of our investing markets. The growth of the equity markets exceeded, even shattered, the twenty-year span of rolling returns and averages since the turn of the century. For the most part, it was too easy to invest in a stock or mutual fund and just hold on and watch it grow. Think back on the easiest times of your life. What were the circumstances? How did you get into that position? What did you learn from those times? This is what I have found in my research: a time of ease is generally not when we as Americans learn our most valuable lessons. So I'm going to change the question for you here. Think about your *tough* times. Did you hit a tough spot at a certain time in your life? Maybe it was something that happened to you before you finished school. Maybe it was after your children were born. Maybe you lost a job. Did you go through a company change? Did you go through a family change? Did you go through a spiritual change?

There seems to be an uncanny way that God shapes us through the tough times so that we actually learn. It's amazing to me how quickly people forget what the tough times teach them as soon as things start to improve again. Remember the famous quote, "Never waste a good tragedy"? You learn more from losing than you ever learn from winning. Winning feels better. Winning is more fun, but what do you really learn? I am convinced you can't truly enjoy winning until you have *failed* at something and *learned* what it takes to win!

I challenge each of you to make a list, right now, before we move on to the Second Key. Make a list of the best times in your life and the toughest times in your life. The key to this exercise is to write down what you really learned during both of these times. My guess is, like our family and most of our friends, your most valuable lessons came from the tough times.

Now, what does this have to do with guaranteed income? How does "*guaranteed income*" sound to you? How would that sound to you in retirement? Where do you find guaranteed income? There are only a few places where this term can actually be used. Social Security is the first place we look. Does anyone actually think the US government would not pay our people their Social Security? Yes, there may be challenges with the amount of money in the system for future generations, but in my humble opinion, there is *no way* the government would let this happen.

The big problem with Social Security is that, in most people's cases, it is simply not enough to retire on, much less to beat inflation with or keep up with the lifestyle that most Americans enjoy. Some of the hardest cases I have witnessed in my career are the people who have only their Social Security payments as income and end up moving in with their children or into a government home later in life. I have never net anyone where that was their first choice in retirement.

The Three Keys to a Truly Happy Retirement

The Social Security Administration sends out a projection statement to each person sixty to ninety days prior to your birthday. I recommend if you are not retired that you make a folder, and every year look for this statement in the mail, and make sure you save it so you can discuss it with your financial advisor. If you cannot find your statement or want more information, please log on to ssa.gov to print a current statement and even see future income modeling and projections.

The other places where you hear *guaranteed income* are company and government pensions. My father-in-law retired from the United States army, and he receives a government pension that sends him a paycheck every month. Many large United States corporations had these types of plans for their employees in the 1960s, 70s, and 80s, but the number of companies who still offer these as benefits are rapidly shrinking each year. Fewer and fewer Americans will have this as a retirement option. People who have pensions *love* them! If you don't believe me, just find someone who *does* have a pension, and ask this person how it feels to get a check every month that can't be outlived. Many pensions are forms of contracts called immediate annuities. These are contracts in which a lump sum of money is given to an insurance company, and the company then provides a lifetime stream of income for either a single-life or a married couple's joint-life; usually the joint-life will have a lower annual or monthly payment because it covers a husband and a wife, and females have longer life expectancies. This concept of payments from an insurance company is what has morphed into the variable-annuity industry we see today. You see, this involved a major change that took place in the financial industry. For over a century, the most financially sound and trusted companies in America were insurance companies, companies that survived the Great Depression: Metropolitan Life, Lincoln Financial, Jefferson Pilot, The Hartford, Prudential, New York Life, Mass Mutual, John Hancock, and others. These companies have been the true backbone of safety in this country. How many of you have life insurance?

Until late in 2008 and early 2009, no person in America had ever lost a minute of sleep worrying about the large life-insurance companies going out of business. The financial crisis of 2008 that our country endured—with the banks and the shenanigans that went on in the mortgage and housing industry—shed light on some of the newer concerns about all things financial, but guess what? All these major insurance companies survived for their policyholders and their stockholders, even AIG. As of this writing, AIG is still in business now, thanks to the United States government and a $185 billion bailout package, but here's what people need to know: whether you agree or disagree with what happened with AIG (a discussion that's not the purpose of this chapter), I plan to show you that none of the policyholders from these companies have missed on claim, death benefit, or annuity payment. I know, because my parents have an annuity contract with AIG's Sun America division as of the writing of this book. AIG got themselves into serious troubles by being the dominant provider of subprime mortgage insurance. These shenanigans with subprime mortgage insurance were so questionable that most of the US states' insurance departments stepped in and said they did not recognize the subprime mortgage insurance as being traditional or as being real insurance. Most people have no idea that each state has an Insurance Commissioner and a state insurance department. These state insurance departments usually conduct actual audits of each insurance company that is licensed to business in their state. They usually do these audits once or twice annually, and in 2008 they were working overtime checking on all these companies. The insurance commissioners from states around the country brought up the fact that the type of insurance AIG was doing with subprime mortgages was different and not as safe or traditional as far as the holding of reserves and traditional insurance practices. The State Commissioners made the industry stop referring to this as traditional insurance, because it did not meet the stringent reserve requirements the life-insurance companies had to keep in their general accounts for policies such as homeowners insurance, automobile insurance, and, yes, life-insurance and annuities. These insurance commissioners actually helped protect people by keeping insurance companies doing only the business that could truly be accounted for and backed by general accounts.

People don't realize that insurance companies have to maintain reserves of capital (that is, extra cash) on the side, through what's called a general account, to cover these policies that they write for individuals and for corporations. These general accounts are established where the assets are placed into them separately from the operating account or, as mot Americans would like to say, the checking account of the insurance company itself.

Insurance company general accounts are public information and, in every state, the state insurance department usually audits them at least once per year. The credit rating agencies such as Standard and Poor's, Moody's, and AM Best, and all the analysts at the brokerage and mutual-fund firms review and issue commentary on the general accounts, in most cases quarterly. Quite frankly, they are the highest-quality bond investments and the most-watched pools of money in the financial word. They're almost always referred to as huge, boring, safe, pools of money.

Why is that? Because if you die, you want your family to collect on your life-insurance policy! Same thing: if you wreck your car or have a fire in your home, we want to know the insurance company has you protected. My personal belief is that they absolutely do. These guarantees are not free, but they are real.

Back in the 1950s, the United States government created something called retirement accounts. They started with retirement accounts for employees of nonprofit organizations such as government entities like school districts, fire departments, and police stations, as well as not-for-profit organizations such as churches, hospitals, and charities. They call these retirement accounts 403(b) accounts and 457 accounts. In our industry, we explain them as being very similar to a 401(k) that is available only to people in the nonprofit corporation world. Millions of Americans have these accounts, and millions of Americans put money aside every month through these plans. The largest provider of these plans in the United States is a company called TIAA-CREF.

The TIAA stands for Teachers Independent Annuity Association. These annuity products were created for the benefit of government employees and not-for-profit employees back in the 1950s. These products are like a personal pension plan. You put money into these plans, and when you are ready to retire, you then take

The Three Keys to a Truly Happy Retirement

your pension or, as we refer to in our industry, annuitization. Once you annuitize one of these accounts or one of these insurance contracts, then the insurance company starts sending you payments that last for a set amount of time—in most cases, your lifetime.

Your can annuitize for specific periods of time such as ten years, fifteen years, or twenty years instead of for a lifetime, but there is generally a trade-off. If you annuitize for only a certain period of time and you're still living afterwards, you get no money. This is not normally an option through these TIAA-CREF annuities, where the government is involved. These were set up and created to provide private or personal pensions for individuals.

Most Americans want no chance of outliving their month paycheck. We use this knowledge to explain the evolution of these products to today's world. Many Americans who funded these plans started in the 1950s and 1960s and saw their accounts start to add up and grow. It is very important to also recognize that the average working American in the 1950s and 1960s saved more money than Americans save today. The average American in the 1950s and 1960s also had a considerably lower level of debt than Americans do at present. Because of these qualities, they wanted to save the money that they had and were earning that was above the contribution limits these 403(b) and 457 accounts would allow.

The government has for many years allowed people to invest in annuities outside of retirement plans. What that means is that the money that you put into an annuity outside of a retirement plan—in something such as a single account for one individual or a join account for a husband and a spouse—are not tax-deductible when you set them up. However, all the earnings in these accounts do grow or accumulate the interest in a tax-deferred manner. What that means is that if you're earning four percent per year for ten years and you do not touch that account, you will not pay taxes on the four percent interest that you earn. However, whenever you get to the point where you need to take income from that account, the interest that you have earned and deferred the taxes on will come out first and be taxable as ordinary income.

There are some other creative ways to get money tax-efficiently out of these products, but

The Three Keys to a Truly Happy Retirement

I'm not going to get too much into details on that. Because people pay the taxes on the earnings that do not go into qualified retirement plans like a 401(k) or a 403(b), the IRS allows all after-tax money or nonqualified investment money to go towards annuities. This is becoming a very hot topic because of multiple reasons, including the fact that people in this country are living longer, and let's face it—our government's debt continues to explode.

These supplemental retirement plans—or supplemental pension plans, or tax-deferred annuities—operate very similarly to a 401(k) or a 403(b) as I just mentioned, because your earnings grow tax-deferred. But one thing you do need to know is that if you try to take money or earnings out of these plans before you turn age 59 ½, you will pay ordinary income taxes, plus a ten percent IRS penalty on all monies earned above your initial contribution.

Our US tax rates were considerably higher in the 1960s and 1970s, so these nonqualified or tax-deferred annuity programs really started to catch on. When the Reagan administration dramatically cut tax rates in the early 1980s, Americans had more to save and to invest, and tax-deferral was still the place to go. Tax rates today are considerably lower than they have been in previous years; however, many people think that there's a strong possibility that we are going to see tax rates increase due to the government's debt situation.

As the annuity industry began to really grow and expand, Americans began to see the markets take off, and these nonqualified annuity accounts grew larger and larger. Many Americans did not have the life expectancy we enjoy today, so as these accounts grew and more people aged with larger balances, they began looking for more protection against market losses.

A common feature of most annuities issued in the 1980s was a death benefit. This was through what's called an insurance rider, which is a feature of an insurance contract where you pay a set amount of money in addition to the normal cost of the insurance, and it guarantees a set value for your family in the case of your death. This rider allowed investors to purchase an annuity (in most cases, variable annuities) and invest in mutual funds for the growth that the investors were becoming accustomed to, while also enjoying the tax-deferral on that growth, and, most importantly, while benefiting from having a guarantee that their beneficiaries could not get back less than what they had invested.

Here's a quick example: A seventy-year-old person invested $100,000 in a variable annuity. Their immediate death benefit is the $100,000 investment. In 1987, the stock market crashed and dropped twenty-two percent in one day. If that $100,000 investment in that variable annuity would have been tied to the Standard and Poor's 500, that account value would have dropped to somewhere around $80,000 that day, depending on how it was invested. If the seventy-year-old owner of this particular annuity passed away the following day, his family or his beneficiaries would have utilized the death benefit rider, and, instead of getting the $80,000 account value like a mutual fund, they would have gotten the full $100,000 back. This benefit quickly caught on, and millions of investors poured money into these annuities so they had tax-deferral for growth and family protection.

There have been many discussions, articles, lawsuits, and so on, about whether these older annuities were actually good for investors. I firmly believe that you always have cases where they were very appropriate, and also where they were possibly not explained properly. Remember an old saying: "There is no perfect investment."

Through the translation of the laws, the changing of people's longevity in our country, and the disappearance of pension plans and pension plans' availability to the workers in America, we've seen the insurance companies start offering something called living benefits. These living benefits have become, in my opinion, the most valuable benefits to investors today who are looking for a way to have guaranteed income in retirement.

Let's take that same example, that $100,000 investment in that variable annuity in 1987 that a day later, after the crash in 2008, dropped to roughly an $80,000 account value. However, the clients today, who, instead of the death benefit, chose the living benefit. Those clients would have been able to start taking a pension income off that $100,000 account even though their account balance showed $80,000, and not only would they have been able to start withdrawing income off that $100,000.00 guaranteed amount, but they would have known and had

The Three Keys to a Truly Happy Retirement

the peace of mind that through that general account that that insurance company keeps, that that paycheck or that pension amount off that $100,000 guarantee would be mailed to them either every month or every quarter for the every year as long as they're alive.

Now think about that. We hear people in America worried and concerned that Social Security may not be around when they get there, but, here's a question: How many people do you know today who are getting their Social Security checks from the government every month and are truly concerned that the government is going to stop sending them their check? They know they are going to get the check. With pensions, a lot of times they were either funded by the company or unfunded by the company, which means that the company promised to pay it, but didn't have the money. Well, folks, here's what you need to know: these insurance companies' annuities with living benefit riders, or these insurance company products called immediate annuities—these are funded pensions for individuals. The money is there; it's allocated in the general account, and if the insurance company totally went out of business, the money in that general account cannot be touched by other corporations with which that insurance company may have had liabilities or debt. The monies in that general account are there to pay out to the policyholders. They're there to make the payments. Guaranteed income and these annuity products are becoming a bigger and bigger part of Americans' retirement plans, because people know that they are living longer and that Social Security is probably not going to be enough. More and more people do not have pensions available for retirement, and they need alternative ways to have the core part of their monthly expenses covered by guaranteed, predictable, reliable income. Think about what my mother-in-law told me at the hospital: "No matter what happens, I have two paychecks for as long as I'm alive."

If you cannot say that, and you know this would be a huge stress relief for your retirement, I suggest you contact your financial advisor and have a detailed discussion with him or her about a true income strategy, and learn exactly how much guaranteed income you will have you when you retire. If your advisor is not comfortable with this discussion, I strongly suggest that you get a second opinion, as more and more advisors are trying to become income specialists for their retired and near-retirement clients. Bonds, stock dividends, and certificate of deposits all have income features, but they can't say that they will pay you an income for as long as you are alive. Only annuities can offer this.

chapter THREE

The 2nd Key to a Truly Happy Retirement

Low or *No* Debt

How many times do we sit paying our monthly bills thinking to ourselves, "Wow, the money goes so fast"? Or do you have this thought: "Hmm, I don't think that this monthly payment that I have to make on this item is really worth what we have?" Or do you have the question, "Did we pay too much for that?" You know debt is such a hot topic in this country, especially due to the recession and everything that's been going on, and there are hundreds of proponents of getting out of debt and staying away from credit cards and the crazy lifestyle that people try and keep up with here in America.

As far as the subject goes, there are books, radio programs, TV shows, and newspaper columns everywhere, all claiming that they know the answer to getting and staying debt-free. There are even companies who charge you to help consolidate or manage debt. Some of these companies who charge you fees to do this are very shady and not reputable, in my opinion. Here is my observation: for the most part, the majority of advice that people have access to on getting out of debt and staying out of debt is right on. Dave Ramsey is one who comes to mind, and, as I have watched his TV show a few times, he in particular seems to be the one person who stands out as giving honest, practical advice on getting out of debt. Most people can do this by just grabbing themselves by the bootstraps and making up their mind! You have to be totally determined to do this. Nobody can help you if you are not committed to eliminating your debt.

The problem comes when these "debt gurus" overstep their qualifications and start giving financial or investment advice. Most of these pundits or TV personalities do not have the true financial education or even the Securities and Exchange Commission and FINRA licenses necessary to provide financial advice on specific investments, portfolios, or custom-tailored plans for individuals. For the most part, these advisors are not qualified. If you want to listen to them on ways to reduce credit-card debt, keep you in check when considering purchasing that big, new SUV, or upgrading and buying another home, or other things that could get you in financial trouble, you know what? It's okay; go right ahead. That is where, in my opinion, these people, these gurus and pundits on debt control serve their best purpose.

That being said, if you're retired currently or if you're near retirement, I want you to ask yourself the following questions: When I'm retired, do I want to have to make a house payment? When I'm retired, do I want a large house payment? When I'm retired, do I want a second mortgage? When we're retired, do we really need two brand-new cars? You see, there are unknowns in retirement that people in their twenties and thirties and forties don't even consider—things like inflation, personal health, health care, health insurance, or location. Where do I live in retirement? Mobility: Can I even get around? Can

Tripp Thompson

I take care of myself? These are real concerns and real issues that lots of people in this country—especially retirees and eldercare people—don't always plan properly for. Imagine the following scenario: You get a notification that your home payment is going to go up twenty percent next year, and you could not sell that house if you wanted to. What would that feel like in retirement? It's almost identical to retirees who are living on a figure—let's say, $20,000 to $30,000 a year—but are paying $200, $300, or $500 a month for their medical prescriptions. You see, younger people, when we hear these scenarios, we think, gosh, I'm glad I don't have to worry about that, or, hopefully that'll be fixed by the time I get that age, or, maybe that will never apply to me. The reality of it is that a lot of elderly people in this country have been getting these notifications of cost increases and cost-of-living increases for quite a few years. We all know what's happening with our country and our government deficit. But also consider that as people in this country age, the companies that provide the benefits and the health insurance continue to get pushed to financial points where, quite candidly, their only real option to appease their stockholders and shareholders is to reduce benefits and cut costs. When they cut costs, often they decrease their participation in what it costs to have the health insurance and to have the medical care and the prescription benefits that a lot of retirees enjoy; and when they do that, it generally raises a retiree's deductibles, co-pays, and occasionally eliminates their health-insurance coverage. If you don't believe that this is a growing problem in our country, just ask around. What you find out might shock you.

You see, we could go on much further in this chapter about debt and staying out of debt, but I am keeping this as simple as possible. Here's why. Debt ruins people's lives when it gets out of control. In retirement, and especially near retirement, this has to be minimal at worst. Go back to my first hard lesson and the story of my father-in-law and my mother-in-law. Because they had no debt and because they had two forms of guaranteed income (the two government pensions), they had no real financial concerns after his heart attack except for getting him well. You see, no mortgage, no credit card, no car, no house, would ever address this properly. Their only bills are for groceries, utilities, telephone and cable, and property taxes. Sounds nice, doesn't it? Here's your only assignment from this second key to a truly happy retirement:

Take out your monthly bills. Every bill you get on a recurring basis, lay out on a large kitchen or dining-room table where you can see every one of them; now, I want you to take the bills that you absolutely must pay, as I'll refer to these as your essential bills or necessary bills. Put them on the left side of the table. Then I want you to take all the other bills, including your mortgage, and put them on the right side (your second or third automobile, maybe, your timeshare or golf club membership). I want you to put those on the right. We're going to call these non-essential bills. Some people think the mortgage is an essential bill, and it absolutely is, depending on your age, but it should not be when you hit retirement age. Do this drill with your mortgage on both sides of the table and watch the difference it would make in retirement if it were eliminated or paid off!

Now here's where the drill takes its most important shape. You need to manually add up each side of the table: the necessary bills or essential bills and then the non-essential bills. See how much different your financial life would be if

The Three Keys to a Truly Happy Retirement

you could greatly reduce or eliminate the non-essential bills. If this does not open your eyes as to what your low to lack of debt situation needs to be, near or in retirement, I'm simply going to say the following: I'll pray for you, because you're going to need help. Remember: a successful retirement or a successful life has nothing to do with your "stuff" —possessions like fancy cars, expensive watches, and designer wardrobes come at a cost. The habits you practice today will be a part of your lifestyle when you retire. People who are no longer working who don't get these habits under control have extreme difficulties realizing that they have a much smaller amount of income than they are accustomed to. Many retirees who suffer from depression are those who couldn't manage these expectations. If you have ever seen retirees who had to drop their country-club memberships because they could no longer afford them, then you would understand what I am trying to impress upon you. A great statistic from the super book *The Millionaire Next Door* claims that the average millionaire never pays more than $300 for a watch! You want your retirement to be similar to a Toyota Camry's reputation: comfortable, efficient, and practical. Please notice I am not talking about being a total frugal hermit. I am not even referring to being "cheap". I am talking about being practical and money-wise. Ask yourself: would driving a newer model Camry or Accord really be any different than driving a BMW or a Mercedes? How much could I save, and what could I do differently with that extra money? You need safe, reliable transportation in retirement, but you most likely do not need a $70,000 vehicle.

If you can't get this under control, I promise you will have problems in retirement, and your emotional challenges could be strenuous. Again, if you are taking the time to read this book, I feel confident that you do not want that scenario to happen. Get this addressed now, so that in retirement you can spend your time on the right things instead of paying bills and pinching pennies. The choice is up to you!

chapter

FOUR

The 3rd Key to a *Truly* Happy Retirement:

Serving Others

The third characteristic of a truly happy retirement is the most rewarding and underemphasized characteristic in history. Have you ever met a wealthy person who is miserable? Have you ever met a physically attractive person who was just not nice to be around? As you remember, the First Key to a *Truly* Retirement is Sufficient Guaranteed Income. The Second Key to a *Truly* Happy Retirement is Low to No Debt. But here it is, folks: The Third and final Key is serving something that *benefits other people*. You can have all the money in the world, but without this activity, without this key, I promise you will never truly know what happiness is. This doesn't mean going off and saving the world. What I'm talking about is spending your time volunteering, helping, driving, cooking, coaching, teaching, preaching, and so on. Find a true activity that gets your energy and attention and your heart in the practice of doing something for someone else's benefit. Most of the time, this means doing something for someone else's benefit without any pay. Do you know someone who volunteers for a charity? How about someone who spends time helping out at church? As I have had this conversation with financial advisors across the country, I love to ask them the following question: Who is your happiest retired client? I ask them to tell me about them. Quite a few times they will say, "I have a client who is not my wealthiest client but is an absolute joy to be around." I ask them to tell me more about these people. They usually tell me a little about their family and maybe what company or industry they're retired from, and then it hits them: this happily retired person is usually doing something for other people. I love to ask, "What do you mean?" The answers are always different but somehow share the same characteristics. I have heard things

The Three Keys to a Truly Happy Retirement

like, "Oh, he's the handyman at church," or, "She's always helping out at the nursing home," or, "They're Sunday school teachers," or, "He's chairman of the local Habitat for Humanity." I have never once heard, "Oh, he's just retired and plays golf." I have heard that statement, but it's *never* been tied to who is your happiest client. I *have* heard, "Oh, they are just loaded wealthy and don't have a care in the world." That specific response tells me that the advisor has no idea how to ask the important questions. You see, with tons of money usually comes tons of responsibility. With tons of responsibility, you can easily find stress. We have all heard people say you can't take it with you, yet we have thousands, even millions, of people in our country who actually try to. The Bible teaches us to serve God with our hearts and minds. If we truly listen to what God tells us, it is to serve him by serving others. By using our physical presence to make a difference in someone else's life, God rewards us with good feelings. Think about a time when someone really needed your help. When you answered the call and you helped someone in need, how did you feel? When we feel good from serving others, I believe that is God's grace.

That's what allows a sense of calm, warmth, and contentment to come over us. Some even refer to those feelings as the Holy Spirit. Why would we feel our best after we have done something that serves another person? Most major religions all have differences and major disagreements about who God is, or if Jesus was actually God's son or just a prophet. They all, however, share a similar teaching that is "Serving Others."

Here's your call. God is telling you someone needs your help. I cannot tell you where to go and where to serve. That is a place where you have to follow your heart and your gut instinct. If you attend a church, you know they need volunteers. If you can drive and have reliable transportation, you know there are people, generally elderly people, who need someone to help drive them to get them from point A to point B, maybe to the grocery store or to a doctor's appointment, or maybe to church. If you can give an hour or two per week, you know there are children's programs in desperate need of help and good role models. If you love sports, most sports programs need coaches and volunteers. If you have a loved one with or have lost a loved one to an illness like cancer, heart disease,

Alzheimer's, diabetes, MS, autism, or any of these kinds of very difficult health issues, there are volunteer organizations based on helping those who are afflicted with these illnesses. If you've been blessed financially, you know there are churches and charities that are in grave need of financial help. I encourage you to do more than financially give. A monetary gift will make you feel very good, but it doesn't always have staying power—unless it's a huge gift! Smile. Writing a big check is not easy, and it is very important, but from what I've observed, physically serving is truly the most rewarding activity.

Ask yourself the following questions and write them down your answers.

- Am I truly happy?

- If I were to retire tomorrow, what would I do to have happiness in my life?

- Where do I know I could help?

- Where do I think I might help?

- What are my God-given skills and talents?

- What could my life experiences do to help teach other people?

- Could telling my story help others?

- Where could I get involved to absolutely benefit someone else?

When it comes to the difference between financial giving and actual physical volunteering, say the following, and feel which one sits better in your heart.

For example, "I gave money to the new church building project," or, "I helped build the new church," or, "I gave money to the cancer society," or, "I volunteer at the cancer society to help those who battle this disease." If you're like me, it's actually the way they sound when you do *both*. Here's why I say that: We all have God-given strengths and talents. Personally, I am not a handyman. I am not talented when it comes to anything to do with engineering or construction projects. So, when those projects are in need, I can volunteer, but I sometimes don't make much difference and honestly don't feel comfortable. In those cases, maybe it's better for me to financially give. When it comes to teaching others and telling Bible stories and sitting down and talking to people about protecting their income and protecting their investments, those are the strengths that God has given me, and I feel called to use those.

Miracles happen every day, but the people who are there are the only ones who actually get to see them happen. When you sit back and reflect on your life, what will you say about you? What will your God say about how you lived your life? What will others say about you? The old saying that only you and God know for sure is absolutely right, but I can testify that the happiest retirees who I have seen in our country have other people who would gladly testify that they walk the walk—that the serve others and give of their time and talents.

Here's the best news. It's not too late for most of us to start if we're not currently serving others. There are over three hundred million people in the United States alone. Imagine if we set an example by serving others. What a difference we could make, one person at a time! You have to answer to the person you see in the mirror and to your maker on your fateful day. Do you want that conversation to be good or bad? Does the answer have any real ramifications? Do you care? I believe you do. Isn't that actually why you are reading this book? I sincerely hope you find this book as an educational starting point.

God has not equipped me to answer all your questions. He certainly has not equipped me to erase your debt or give you a lifetime pension. He hasn't even told me where you need to go to serve others. He did, however, give me the guidance and the life experiences to prepare this book. I believe in my heart that God wants us to be free to serve others. He doesn't want us to worry about money, and he certainly does not want us to be a slave to possessions and debt. He does want us to do as he says and follow him. We do this by not serving two gods. We serve him: not ourselves, and certainly not money.

Conclusion

The 1st Key to a *Truly* Happy Retirement:

Sufficient Guaranteed Income

Have the courage to research ways to protect your current and future income. Ask the right questions about your financial plan, investment assets, and your advisor.

The 2nd Key to a *Truly* Happy Retirement:

Low to No Debt

Have the tough conversation about your current debt situation. Make the tough decisions now, so they are easier later and not represent a significant hurdle in your retirement comfort
and well being.

The 3rd Key to a *Truly* Happy Retirement:

Serving Others

Have the courage to follow your heart and serve others. They need you. God is calling you to take action and to enjoy the blessings he pours on you for doing good deeds for others.

I want to thank you for taking the time to read this book. I want to leave you with this:

I pray for you, and that your family situation can somehow be improved by the stories and 3 Keys discussed here.

I also pray for your life and retirement success.

And lastly, I hope when I meet some of you in my travels, you can share with me your success stories of a *truly* happy retirement.

Thanks again, and God bless.

E.S. "Tripp" Thompson III

www.ingramcontent.com/pod-product-compliance
Lightning Source LLC
Chambersburg PA
CBHW061518180526
45171CB00001B/239